Discovering
Hydroponic
Gardening

From Earth to Water

Discovering Hydroponic Gardening

By
ALEXANDRA COLLINS DICKERMAN
JOHN DICKERMAN

Illustrated by
TYRELL COLLINS

Published by
WOODBRIDGE PRESS PUBLISHING COMPANY
Santa Barbara, California 93111

Published by
WOODBRIDGE PRESS PUBLISHING COMPANY
Post Office Box 6189
Santa Barbara, California 93111

Copyright © 1975 by Alexandra Dickerman and John Dickerman

LIBRARY OF CONGRESS CATALOG CARD NUMBER: 75-17274

INTERNATIONAL STANDARD BOOK NUMBER: 0-912800-19-4

Published Simultaneously in the United States and Canada

PRINTED IN THE UNITED STATES OF AMERICA

dedicated to the memory of our father, George E. Collins with love to our wives, and our family

Contents

Part IV: Hydroponic Specialties and Recipes

Part V: Serious Thoughts

Part VI: Books and Sources

Preface

We discovered hydroponic gardening almost accidentally. There are many other people who would like to grow their own food but don't know about this wonderful system, so our book is written as a nontechnical introduction to the rewarding world of hydroponics for everyone who wants his own easy-care garden.

Originally, we thought it was necessary to live on a farm to have all the fresh, natural foods we wanted. Now, however, we have found that it is possible to live even in a small city apartment and grow a bountiful supply of vegetables, fruits, and flowers—hydroponically.

We hope that anyone who wants to garden with little space, time, and labor will discover this system to be as rewarding and exciting as it has been for us.

Part I:
Introduction

What Is
Hydroponic Gardening?

This book about our gardening experiences covers all the basic ideas and methods you will need for starting your own simple hydroponic system. You may want to begin with nothing more than a flower pot. Eventually you may find that a hydroponic greenhouse best fits your needs. Whatever techniques and equipment you decide to use, we are sure you will be delighted with your hydroponic adventures.

Hydroponics is a centuries-old but still little-known method of gardening. This highly efficient, intensified growing technique is so effective it is even planned for use by American astronauts in future space shuttle programs.

A bountiful tomato crop from high-density planting in a homemade hydroponic growing tray.

In hydroponics, an inert soil substitute—like gravel—is used and a balanced nutrient solution is fed to plants daily, allowing them to grow bigger and faster in smaller spaces than they ever could in an ordinary garden.

For example, hydroponically grown tomatoes ripen in 8-10 weeks and produce four to five times as much fruit as similar plants grown in the same amount of space in the soil. Cucumbers ripen in 5 days and bibb lettuce is ready in 40 days, seedling to harvest.

Hydroponic gardening conserves water and fertilizer, which are reused—over and over. Insect and disease problems are minimized since sterile, nonorganic growing mediums are used in place of soil and plants are usually grown indoors or in a screened greenhouse.

It has been our experience that the convenience and efficiency of hydroponic gardening makes it an ideal way to raise family crops. We have been able to produce all the vegetables and flowers and many of the fruits we want any season of the year. We have found that home gardening doesn't have to require a great amount of time, effort, or space. Even a very small place is big enough for a hydroponic garden!

A flower pot is just right for a season full of hydroponically grown strawberries.

Part II:

Frustration Farming!

"A Place in the Country"

The city was dirty and noisy and we wanted to move to the country. We were able to find a small, rural community on the coast just the size and location we felt was ideal and we bought an old farm—run-down and cheap.

The farm was part of an old pig ranch and fences ran every which way, around the house, around the garden, through the pasture, down the hill, all sprawling and broken. The house was fairly small and the roof leaked. There was only one small space heater and there were no gas lines for the gas stove.

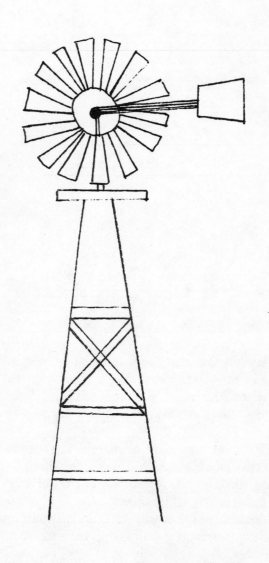

John had to hook the stove to a propane tank, which meant a gusty flame, but it was handier than a wood stove. And I took to wearing the electric blanket for a bathrobe.

We liked the idea that there was no TV reception in our small valley basin. We anticipated a simple life of clean air, hard work, and good food. We planned to have fresh fruits and vegetables from our garden, fresh eggs, and maybe even a milk cow.

Our objective was to develop an extensive organic plot and we had hopes of ultimately developing an autonomous system, powered by the old windmill, solar energy, and a small pond for fish and hydroelectric power.

Our first job was to clear a space for the garden. The pigs had years ago routed the land and then a crab type of bermuda grass had invaded the place. We set off about a 50- by 100-foot area and started to work restoring the soil.

We loaded our truck with horse manure, free for the digging from a nearby horse ranch. The digging was strenuous and unpleasant and it took us weeks to finally unload the truck. Meanwhile it stood in the pasture. Then it rained. It took us days to dig the truck out of the mud and then days longer to unload it and we were muddy and grimy by the time we finished the job.

After that we decided to build up our own compost pile. Into it we threw all the weeds, wet garbage and manure we could find and waited about four weeks for it to ripen, turning it weekly. This compost was then mixed into the garden earth with an old rototiller the previous owners had left. John looked as if he were on a vibrating machine digging away at the tenacious crabgrass.

Unfortunately, that grass seemed to proliferate each time we rototilled. It must have been a grass that propagated at each broken segment, spreading more and more long, deep tendrils throughout the garden. We battled the grass for the entire time we lived on the farm.

To complete the farm-like atmosphere of our pastoral retreat, we collected roosters—and even a donkey from the local pound. Then we bought geese and laying hens at the "hay, feed, and seed" store. The hens produced wonderful eggs. And they were good a producing a high-nitrogen fertilizer we added to our compost bed.

But rest of the animals we collected turned out to to require a lot of feed and attention for little reward. The donkey was a master at escaping and finally one morning we simply returned him to the pound.

An Organic Garden

Our three and one-half acre farm was located about seven miles from the ocean and the land was a good, rich, sandy loam. Despite the problems of the bermuda grass and the stripping the pigs had done, we had hopes for great productivity from our garden. By this time we had prepared the soil and were ready with seeds we had selected and sent away for all the winter. We had tomatoes, peas and beans, corn, lettuce, onions, cucumbers, carrots, radishes, summer squash, and melons. The previous owners had a grape vine and some tomato bushes already growing heartily.

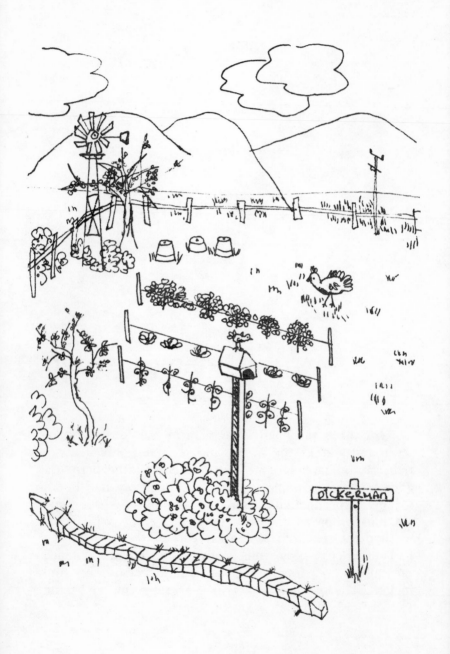

We also ordered praying mantises and ladybugs to keep down the insects, instead of using toxic chemicals in our organic garden. The ladybugs arrived in a small box. The morning they were delivered, we took them out to the garden and released them. Then, there on the bottom of the box we saw a notice: "These ladybugs should be released only at night or they will fly away." They did!

ladybug ladybug

We didn't have much better luck with the praying mantises, which arrived in egg-case clusters, with instructions to attach them to the trees around the property. The cat got the first one and a few blew off in the wind. The rest remain to this day we are told, unhatched.

During the winter we bought bare-root trees. Now we had everything. There was a pear, a peach, a plum, and an apricot tree. Unfortunately, however, the donkey pulled out two of the trees and the rest caught a leaf-curl disease which stripped the blossoms. We had planted an avocado tree and covered it each night to protect it from the cold, but still it didn't survive. The only tree to bear fruit was an ancient crab apple that had grown in the pasture for years.

Meanwhile the crabgrass was busy creeping into the garden. It inched out the marigold border I had planted to discourage the insects (a hint from our organic gardening book) and on into the garden. All of our weeding seemed to be hopeless and that grass spread throughout the garden, still vigorous after we suffered on our hands and knees to clean it out.

Another threat to the garden was the animals. The hens got loose through a hole in the fence the donkey had made and had a holiday with the new corn. The geese made a mess of the peas and beans, a wild rabbit ate the radishes and carrots, and our dog finished things off chasing a deer that had stopped by to taste the lettuce. He trampled down the tidy rows of string and the name tags marking each vegetable, leaving pure chaos. We did harvest a few tomatoes and some peas but the garden was, for the most part, a disaster.

Our Great
Pine Tree Flop

During our first year on the farm we also tried to grow trees from seedlings in addition to our vegetable garden. The state of California offered pine tree seedlings to qualifying growers at very reasonable prices. We ordered a thousand, mainly to use as a windbreak around the property. We also felt the trees would make an esthetic improvement to the land and provide an enclosure of privacy for the farm.

We discovered that one thousand is a lot of seedlings to plant along the periphery of the land. One by one we dug little holes and carefully tamped down each tiny tree.

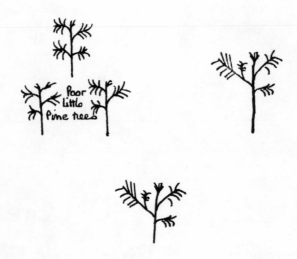

Then we had the job of keeping the trees watered. With all the water hoses connected we could just reach the furthermost limits of the land. The dry, sandy soil absorbed great quantities of water and the job of watering the seedlings took hours. We weren't sure how often the trees required watering and after we discovered the enormity of the job we began to assume that the rain had soaked the soil. Pines can grow without being watered in forests so, we reasoned, our seedlings didn't need to be watered very often either.

Then a scale insect attacked the big Monterey pines around the property and at the same time cut down about a third of the seedlings. Some more died of exposure and the wind. Others dried up. Of the thousand, our total crop, after one year, added up to about 50 little trees.

Although we had been aware of the danger of insects attacking our garden, we were really taken by surprise by other problems: animals, weeds, disease, and weather. The tremendous effort we had made to condition the soil and to seed and maintain our farm that year proved to be all but fruitless. We were disappointed with our gardening results but we were determined to devise more successful and satisfactory growing techniques for our next venture.

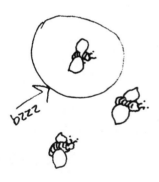

Part III:
Discovering Hydroponics

Discovering Hydroponics

Amid the frustrations of our efforts at growing food from the soil, we noticed that I seemed to have more success with my pots of herbs and spices on the porch than we had with our garden. The pots were naturally easier to plant and maintain. I didn't have to cultivate the soil—it came from a planting mix package. Nor did I have the problems of weeds and disease. By putting the pots in a sheltered place I protected them from weather conditions and they were certainly easy to water with a pail from the kitchen. There was a minimum of danger from insects and animals since the pots were

placed on the porch and I could keep an eye on them. The potted herbs certainly flourished—compared with our farming experience—with just water and, on occassion, some fertilizer.

This gave us the idea that container growing must be a far easier method of gardening.

Nearby, a hydroponic greenhouse was being constructed for growing off-season tomatoes under contract

Success! My pots of herbs flourished with little effort—our first clue that hydroponic gardening was the way to go.

to a local grocery chain. We studied their system and did some research of our own, experimenting with the hydroponic techniques at home.

Essentially, we discovered hydroponic gardening to be something like my herb pots: a means of growing things under controlled conditions to eliminate the problems of unforeseen or uncontrollable natural forces. Using this system it was now possible to grow vegetables, fruits, flowers, and herbs year-round, using a minimum of water and little labor. Such chores as weeding and

Marjoram

cultivating, composting, and stooping row after row to tend the garden were entirely eliminated.

The hydroponic technique, we learned, uses mineral nutrients in an inert growing medium. Instead of dirt, a clean white "popped" granite product, perlite, is most frequently used. The nutrients are dissolved in water so when you water you also feed the plants. The granite simply provides root support.

Our first miniature hydroponic garden—such pride in picking a fresh salad right out of my own dining room!

We couldn't wait to build our own small indoor hydroponic box, trying the methods of the commercial growers, but on a miniaturized scale. We filled our box with perlite—from a garden supply house—and planted seed lettuce, chives, and tomatoes for the kitchen and marjoram, mint, and nasturtium for fun. We bought a prepared formula fertilizer and used a heating cable beneath the box to aid early germination.

Within three weeks all the seeds were up and in three months all the plants were mature. We had done all the growing indoors using a simple growing light. John hooked up a small pump and a timer so all the maintenance was automatic. All I had to do was change the nutrient solution every two weeks.

Imagine my pride the first time I picked a fresh salad for my guests from my own dining room garden!

Our first hydroponic experience has led us to devise various other systems. We have made special containers for propagation, decorative boxes for house plants, and vegetable gardens for indoors and out.

Each new project has been successful and rewarding, surrounding us with the constant enjoyment of growing plants we might have otherwise missed because of a lack of time, space, or energy.

Hearty hydroponic cabbage, lettuce, and much more in our year-round garden.

Advantages of
Hydroponic Gardening

We now have discovered, that it isn't necessary to live on a farm to grow your own food. With hydroponics it is possible to live anywhere and grow a substantial supply of vegetables. With a small yard, you can grow all the vegetables to feed your family season after season, year-round.

To grow vegetables for a family of four by conventional methods requires a plot about 50 feet square. To grow them hydroponically requires only about a 10- by 12-foot space. We knew that the work of a 50- by 50-foot plot is practically a full time job. But with the small hydroponic system, only a couple of hours a week at the most are needed.

Our interest in gardening has been based primarily on our interest in good nutrition, our preference for organically grown foods without harmful chemicals, and our great delight in serving plump, freshly picked treats ripe from the garden.

From our first attempts at organic gardening we resolved to avoid toxic chemicals, poisons, and sprays. Now, using the hydroponic method, it has become unnecessary to use any harmful agents since there are no insects or weeds present in the disease-free growing environment.

If the plant nutrients used are of the purest and highest quality, all the necessary nutrients for sturdy plant growth will be available to be absorbed directly by the plants as they need them.

Furthermore, the water required is tremendously minimized since, in a hydroponic garden, it is recycled. There is no waste or runoff or loss of nutrients. The plants will absorb all the important nutrients—naturally—and grow into highly nutritious food.

Plants germinate faster than ever before under the special hydroponic conditions, they grow bigger in smaller spaces, and they are lush and delicious.

Our experience with hydroponic gardening has been exciting and rewarding. We have had such success with these new gardening techniques that we have been able to experiment, growing different types of plants, developing hybrid strains, growing flowers to eat in

Tomatoes starting to grow tall (left), leaving the sun (or growing lights) to low-growing plants.

String beans thrive in our window-box hydroponic "garden."

salads, making poultices and cosmetics from vegetables, and growing special ornamental specimens to preserve and display in our home.

Hydroponic gardening has made growing so simple and efficient that we have been able to spend our time having fun with the garden products instead of using most of our time and energy on the growing process itself.

We have experimented with, and developed hydroponic methods which provide all we had hoped for from our ill-fated outdoor garden. Perhaps, with more time and energy we could have achieved the same results in the garden, but we have been so delighted with hydroponic growing that we have continued to research and develop hydroponic techniques instead.

We sold the farm and moved to a medium sized city. Now we are busy developing indoor systems and outdoor systems, growing all varieties of seedlings, vegetables, herbs, and even grains hydroponically, summer and winter, in our small back yard.

Sunshine

CO_2

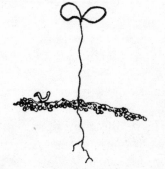

Phosphorus ↑ Nitrogen
Potassium
trace minerals

Your Choice of
Hydroponic Methods

Basically hydroponics is a system which uses a water solution to provide plant nutrients instead of growing them in soil. The plants absorb all the nutrients they need from a mineral mixture dissolved in water and fed directly to their roots.

Plants have several basic requirements for survival. They need potassium, phosphorous, and nitrogen, plus several trace minerals. In normal soil culture, potassium, phosphorous, and trace minerals are provided from the earth. Irrigation water dissolves these nutrients and delivers them to the plant roots. Nitrogen is provided by decaying organic matter. In hydroponics, these minerals are all supplied in solution.

Plant roots also need oxygen to allow iron assimilation. If oxygen were not available the plants would become anemic and eventually die. In hydroponics, root aeration is supplied through the growing medium. Gravel or coarse sand can be used but we prefer sponge rock (perlite) or vermiculite—all available from farm, garden, or hydroponics supply houses.

Simple and easy hydroponic gardening. This small growing tray is flooded twice a day just by raising the container of nutrient solution. It flows through the small, plastic tube you see connecting them. Set the container down and the solution flows back in ready for reuse.

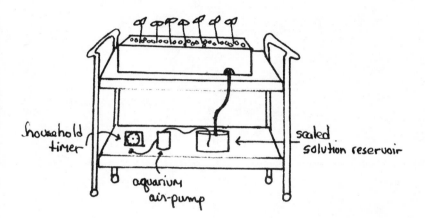

Flooding Method

The objective is to keep the growing medium damp at all times but to allow plenty of oxygen for the roots. All this may be accomplished by several methods.

The most popular method is to flood the growing medium one to three times a day for a period of one-half to two hours at a time. The rest of the time, the roots have oxygen available through the growing medium. After flooding, the water is allowed to drain back into the solution reservoir for reuse later. The flooding process can be done automatically, using a pump and a timer.

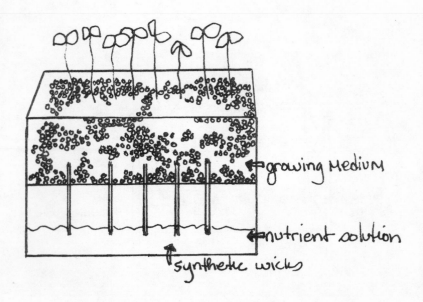

growing medium

nutrient solution

synthetic wicks

wick watering system
(pretending we have xray vision)

Wick Watering Method

Another method, instead of flooding, is to keep the growing medium damp by using a wick watering system. A synthetic fiber wick draws the water solution into the growing medium, allowing both moisture and air to continuously feed the plant.

Drip Irrigation Method

Still another hydroponic technique is drip irrigation, in which the plants are grown in a perlite/peat moss medium. They are watered with the nutrient solution daily, using only enough water so that all the moisture is absorbed by the growing medium and the plants, leaving little or no runoff.

A hydroponic drip irrigation system dispenses nutrient solution into the growing trays or buckets, but does not recycle it.

Standing Solution Method

Water, fertilizer, and oxygen can also be provided to the plant roots by growing them directly in the nutrient solution. Root aeration is then provided by bubbling air into the solution.

Each of these methods has been used with success. The choice of techniques depends on the space, time, money, and preference of the grower. The drip irrigation system is excellent, but requires automatic equipment. Probably the simplest beginning method is the flooding system. Wick watering is best for starting seeds.

Starting Plants from Seed

Germinating from seed, ordinarily a tricky process, is almost foolproof using the hydroponic method. The satisfaction and economy of gardening with plants you have started yourself makes this a major advantage of hydroponic growing.

Your first basic vegetable garden might include simple seeds such as tomatoes, lettuce, cabbage, and brussel sprouts. You should begin with a box about 12 by 20 inches in size, with plenty of drainage holes in the bottom. Fill the box with a medium perlite. Then plant your seeds,

Here's how to make your first simple hydroponic garden. First drill holes in the bottom of a 12"x 20" plastic tray (on one end) for drainage. Next, fill the tray with perlite from your garden shop. Plant your seeds. Keep moist until they sprout. Then feed every four to seven days with a nutrient solution (described later in the book). Collect solution in a bucket for reuse. Hydroponic gardening can be that simple!

spacing them about two inches apart and to the depth indicated on the seed packet. Water gently, trying not to disturb the seeds. Keep them moist and at room temperature. When the plants grow two leaves, start watering daily, using a weak solution—about half normal strength —of hydroponic plant nutrient, available at your nursery or hydroponics supply house.

Keep your plants supplied with sun or use an ordinary fluorescent light if you don't have a sunny spot.

When seeds are germinating, the first two leaves are produced from the nutrients in the seed itself. The second pair of leaves and all additional growth comes from the nutrient solution, sun, and carbon dioxide in the air.

The first two leaves are nourished by the seed itself.

The second set of leaves and subsequent growth must come from nutrients supplied to the plant.

You can start seedlings much cheaper then you can buy plants for
transplanting. Lift them carefully from your starting tray or flower pot
with a dull knife and plant them where you want them to mature.

You can buy a wick-fed seed-starting "greenhouse" like this at many
garden shops and hydroponics supply houses (see sources in back of
book).

After all plants have three sets of leaves, gently remove them from the growing bed, using a dull knife, and gently transplant to a permanent spot in your hydoponic garden or wherever you want them to mature.

There are several good indoor seedling-starting "greenhouses" on the market. Some have a wick system for automatic watering and fertilizing, so all you do is change the solution periodically.

Make Your Own Hydroponic System

You will find it amazingly easy to make any of the several hydroponic growing systems, for almost any container around the house can be converted into a hydroponic growing system.

Flower Pot Hydroponics

A flower pot is the simplest sort of hydroponic container since it already has a hole at the bottom. Plastic dishpans and cat-litter trays also make good containers if you drill holes for adequate drainage.

Even Lexa thinks hydroponic gardening is fun—child's play!

That's Alexandra showing how one feeding a day with nutrient solution makes the tomatoes flourish.

Since, in hydroponics, the roots are fed directly with nutrients, they don't have to dig down to find their food. This means that much less space is used for hydroponic plants. Full-sized 3-to 4-foot tomato plants may be grown in a flower pot and bear delicious fruit if you simply stake the plants for support.

After the plants have started, the main consideration is to water them daily with a nutrient solution. This

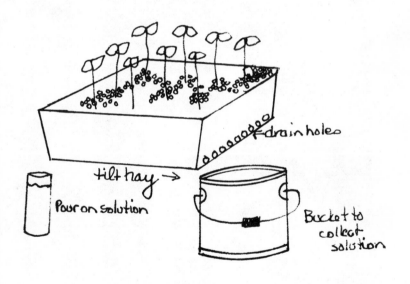

Manual Tray System

Beautiful hydroponic tomatoes!

solution may be collected in a container and recycled, saving materials (and money). Or drain it into your garden if your system is used outside.

Your growing system may be left two to three days at a time, now and then, if the air isn't too hot and dry, but neglecting it longer will kill the plants.

A Wick-Fed System

If you don't want to take the time to water your growing system yourself, you can use a wick-fed system. For this you need two trays, one on top of the other. In the lower tray, place the nutrient solution. The growing medium, perlite, and the plants go in the top tray. A wick draws up the solution and feeds it through a small hole to the perlite in the top tray.

Use a synthetic fabric to make your wicks. We discovered that organic fibers will eventually rot in the water. Use nylon, polyester, or rayon. Test one end of a thin 6-inch-long piece of fabric in water to see if it draws water to moisten the entire piece.

Drill small holes about three inches apart in the bottom of the top planting tray and thread pieces of your wick fabric through the holes down into the water solution in the bottom tray.

Fill the upper tray with a vermiculite or perlite growing medium and wet it well to start the wick action. Then let the wicks do the watering for you, replacing the water solution every two weeks.

Wick systems will build up salts in the growing medium through evaporation. Since this will eventually

Here's the principle of wick-watering—you can watch the wick draw up the water.

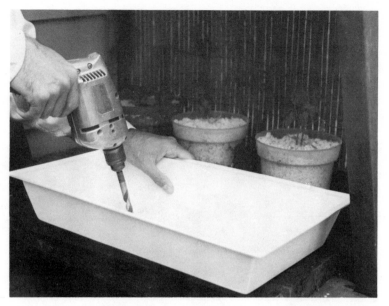

To make a wick-watering system, drill holes in an even pattern about three to four inches apart in the bottom of a plastic tray.

Insert wicks (shaped like those shown here) into the holes, pull through, leaving an inch or so showing in the tray.

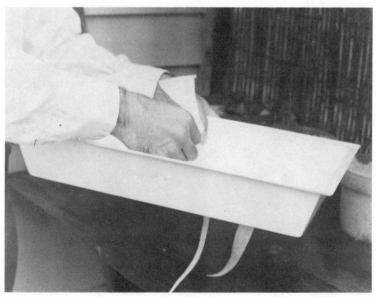

Fill the tray with perlite from your garden shop and set it on top of another tray filled with nutrient solution, supporting it as shown.

Plant your garden! Seeds or transplants—the wicks will draw up the solution, keeping the medium moistened for excellent plant growth.

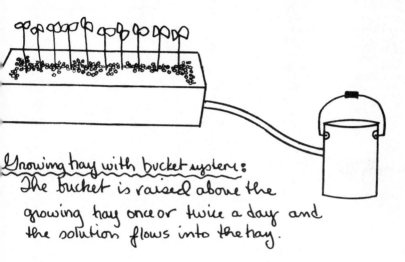

Growing tray with bucket system:
The bucket is raised above the
growing tray once or twice a day and
the solution flows into the tray.

hibit plant growth, the growing medium must be
oroughly flushed and cleaned with tap water every
o months.

Flooding System

You can make another type of growing system with
tray and a bucket. For this method you will need a
astic dishpan or kitty-litter tray, a bucket, and three
et of plastic tubing. Use epoxy glue for connecting the
stem as in the accompanying illustration. Once a day,
t up the bucket so the solution goes through the hose
wn into the growing tray. Leave the bucket up on
shelf or table until all the solution has run into the
ay. After about two hours lower the bucket so that the

solution can drain out of the tray back into the bucket—
ready to be used again tomorrow!

Automating Your System

It is also possible to build an automatic system. One
of the simplest is the air pump system. A simple aquarium
pump is used to move the solution from the reservoir
to the growing tray. The reservoir is an airtight container. Air is pumped into it and the pressure forces
the solution up into the aquarium bed. When the pump
is turned off, the solution drains back down to the
reservoir.

An inexpensive automatic electric timer may be used
to turn on the pump for two hours each day. After
it pumps the solution, it pumps air bubbles which aerate
the growing medium and hold the solution in the growing
bed.

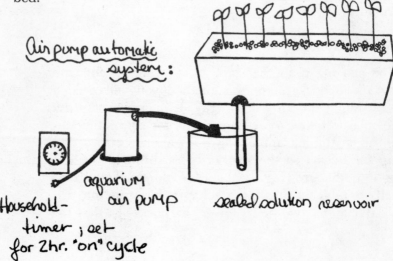

air pump automatic system:

Household-timer; set for 2hr. "on" cycle

aquarium air pump

sealed solution reservoir

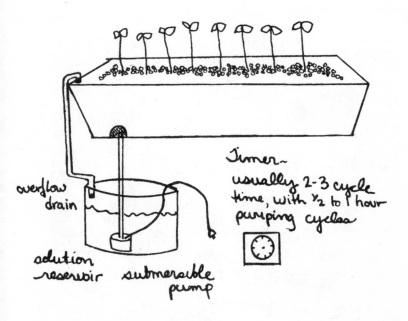

Timer—
usually 2-3 cycle
time, with ½ to 1 hour
pumping cycles

overflow
drain

solution
reservoir   submersible
pump

Water pump automatic system

A more expensive and sophisticated automatic system uses a submersible pump to move the solution instead of using a sealed reservoir. Most commercial and family-sized greenhouses use this type of pump, which can pump two to three cycles a day. It takes the solution from the reservoir into the growing bed for 15 to 20 minutes at a time. A drain positioned about one inch from the top of the growing medium prevents the water from overflowing and algae from forming.

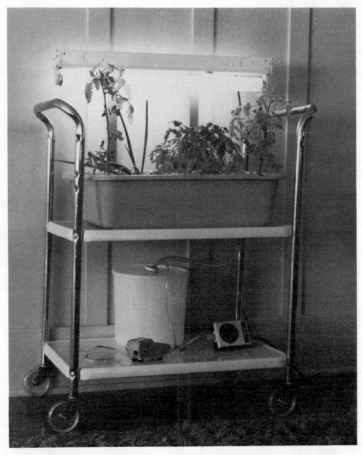

See those fluorescent light tubes? They keep plants growing indoors on this automatic hydroponic grow-cart—with the same results as actual sunlight outdoors!

Ready-Made Hydroponics Systems

Besides these homemade methods, there are several excellent commercial systems available in a variety of sizes, including an indoor grow-cart, a patio model, and a walk-in family sized greenhouse. We have found that these are excellent investments since growing is always successful and effortless. We have both an indoor cart and a outdoor greenhouse in constant, year-round use providing us with off-season, sweet, ripe, and delicious foods.

There are many hydroponic growing aids available. Here is an outdoor growing bed, sheltered by partial "greenhouse" wall.

What Plants Eat

There has been some controversy among dedicated organic gardeners concerning the quality of the hydroponic crop. These gardeners feel that some trace minerals may be missing from hydroponically grown vegetables.

We have found that a carefully formulated nutrient mixture contains all the elements known to be needed for healthy plant growth and we believe our harvests are as fine as those of the best organic gardens.

As we mentioned earlier, all plants need food: primarily they need hydrogen, oxygen, carbon dioxide, nitrogen, phosphorous, and potassium, plus trace minerals such as sulphur, calcium, magnesium, iron, and carbon.

Oxygen is supplied in the water; carbon dioxide, in the air. The rest of the elements are supplied by the nutrient solution. Various mineral salts are mixed to provide the proper proportions of the needed elements.

We have found, however, that mixing the proper nutrient solution is not worth the work involved for the home gardener and we prefer to buy one of the good commercial mixes available from garden or hydroponics

Hydroponic nutrient mixes are available from many suppliers and are much more convenient than mixing your own. One teaspoon of most plant nutrient mixes makes a gallon of hydroponic solution.

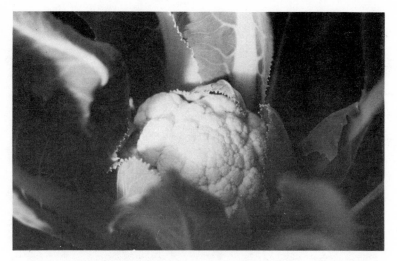

We have experimented with many kinds of food plants in our hydroponic trays—almost all of them do very well.

supply houses (See some addresses in the back of this book.) Among the best are:

Acorn Plant Food
Hyponex
Dr. Chanteleir
Rapid-Gro
Eco-Grow
Bridwell's Mix

It is always important to read and follow the directions on the nutrient mixture package carefully. Usually one teaspoon of nutrient is dissolved in one gallon of water.

Overfertilizing will burn out your plants. For starting seedlings, dilute your solution to half strength and gradually increase the dose as the plants get bigger.

Using a good nutrient solution is the key to hydroponics. Regular, careful feeding of your plants produces optimum growth.

We plant vegetables very close together for maximum production of food. Since you are supplying the nutrients, roots do not need to wander far in search of them.

Alexandra can grow the flowers she loves any season of the year with her indoor hydroponic growing trays.

Where Plants Grow

Soil, as such, is made up of small bits of inert material and it serves first of all to provide anchorage for plants. In hydroponics, this function can be served by a variety of materials.

We generally use medium perlite or sponge rock for starting seeds. Coarse sponge rock makes a good, light-weight medium for growing plants. Both of these are available in bags at garden shops or hydroponic supply houses.

Basically, a good growing medium should have the ability to hold moisture while allowing root aeration. Also, the material should be clean and free of organic materials that will decompose.

Some Common Growing Mediums

Pea Gravel:	Good for large home systems.
Coarse Sand:	Heavy to carry home but good.
Perlite:	Good for small home systems.
Vermiculite:	Fair for small systems, but tends to hold too much water.
Sawdust:	OK, but tends to decay
and/or woodchips:	with extended use.
Cinders:	Good, if available in your area.

Many growing media will work. Here a tomato plant gets a healthy start in ordinary pea gravel.

Light for Dark Corners

If you are growing indoors you may want to use a grow-light. Even with a sunny window your indoor plants don't get as much sun as they would outside and a grow-light provides a good source of the necessary light.

Although there are special commercial grow-lights, we have found regular fluorescent lights produce virtually the same results.

A small growing tray (dishpan size) will require two 24-inch lights, 40 watts each. These should be left on 10 to 16 hours a day and should be at a height of no more than two feet above the growing bed. It's a good idea to devise some sort of shade—tinfoil or plastic—to deflect the light downward.

If your lights have "starters" or "quick-start fixtures" (ask at the hardware store) you may automate them with an inexpensive household timer. Just set the timer for a 12-hour cycle and plug the lights into it.

A grow-light—a special kind widely available, or ordinary fluorescent tubes—makes it possible to start plants indoors or on a shaded patio. Here a commercially available starting tray is being used.

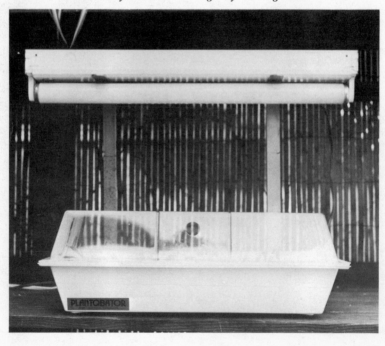

Year-Round Fresh Vegetables

We have been delighted to discover that almost any vegetable will grow hydroponically. We grow what we like to eat. If something doesn't grow well we take it out and keep experimenting.

Miniature and small-sized vegetables are especially good in a hydroponic garden. Beans and peas, eggplant and cherry tomatoes, onions, radishes, carrots, and cucumbers are our favorites as well as most herbs.

You will find that most things will grow except plants

Growd your plants for maximum use of space in your hydroponic garden. You will be amazed at the amount of food you can grow all year in very little space.

that require a dry environment. We are all pioneers in hydroponics, and while we can provide a list of what grows best, you will find it's more rewarding to experiment yourself. Assume everything will grow and you will be right most of the time. Here are a few ideas we have found to be useful for growing hydroponic vegetables:

Start all vegetables in your seed-starting "greenhouse" or a seeding tray to avoid confusion in your growing bed.

Plant several seeds and then select the strongest to transplant when they are small but well-started (four to six leaves).

Crowd your plants into the growing bed for maximum yields, disregarding the seed packet instructions, since the roots don't need as much room as they would in soil.

Plant root crops next to leafy crops, like carrots next to chard and turnips next to spinach.

Plant short leafy vegetables in the partial shade of large crops—such as lettuce next to tomatoes and radishes in the shadow of the towering corn.

As one plant yields food and is ready to be harvested, plant a new one right next to it.

Some planning of your planting scheme is desirable. Here a root crop (onions) is planted next to a leaf crop (lettuce).

Suggested Indoor Growing Bed Plan

cherry tomatoes | leaf lettuce | cherry tomatoes
radishes
HERBS | Spinach | HERBS
carrots
green onions
turnips (for greens)
swiss chard
watercress

Suggested Ratio of Greenhouse Growing Bed Plan

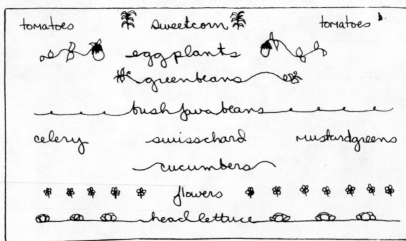

tomatoes | Sweetcorn | tomatoes
eggplants
greenbeans
bush java beans
celery | swisschard | mustardgreens
cucumbers
flowers
head lettuce

Many shapes and sizes. If you want a full-scale home hydroponic greenhouse, you can surely find what you want.

Part IV:
Hydroponic Specialties
and Recipes

Your Own
Mushroom Crop

One of the most rewarding crops in our hydroponic garden has been mushrooms. We have enjoyed finding recipes for our abundant supply of that exotic, elegant fungus, otherwise so expensive we would use them only for special meals.

Since they are a fungus, mushrooms don't grow like ordinary plants. They live on decaying organic material.

We raise our hydroponic mushrooms in a compost of sawdust and hay which has been activated and decomposed with the aid of hydroponic fertilizers. Organic mushrooms are usually grown in a horse manure compost.

We make our hydroponic mushroom compost in a cylinder made of chicken wire about the size of a garbage can. This is the formula we have found to work best:

    5 lb hay
    2 lb sawdust
    1 lb ammonium sulphate
    1 lb superphosphate
    ½ lb urea

Add enough water to moisten the mixture completely. Then, every five days dump out the compost, mix it up, add some more water and replace it in the cylinder. During the second mixing add:

    1 lb calcium carbonate
    1 lb gypsum powder

Always keep the compost damp; mix it every five days for a total of three weeks.

Now the compost is ready for use. Fill your hydroponic growing tray with it. Add a mushroom spawn, available from most seed companies. Keep the bed cool, damp, and dark; for instance under your sink, in the basement, or in the garage.

In about three weeks, your compost bed will become permeated with little white fibers, the mycelium. At this point, cover the bed with damp sand or perlite about one inch deep to bring on the mushrooms. Within a few

days, the mushrooms should appear and will last six to eight weeks if you keep the bed damp. Now all you do is keep picking and eating!

We like to dry the mushrooms—if we have any extra after our friends have been supplied with plenty.

Drying Mushrooms

Dried mushrooms retain almost the full mushroom flavor. They must be soaked before using. Clean them and spread them out on trays in a slightly warmed oven until they are dry and shriveled. When cool, store them in an airtight container.

Here are some of our favorite mushroom recipes:

Mushrooms with Herbs

    1 lb sliced mushrooms
    1 chopped onion
    ¼ cup oil
    ¼ cup bouillon or stock
    1 tsp each oregano, parsley, marjoram

Cook onions in oil until lightly browned. Add mushrooms, tossing until well-coated with oil. Add the stock and the herbs. Cover and bake at 350° for 20 minutes.

Greek Mushrooms

1 lb small mushrooms
1½ tbsp wine vinegar
¼ cup olive oil
1 clove crushed garlic
parsley, marjoram, and salt

Add oil, vinegar, and herbs to a saucepan. Barely cover with water and simmer until herbs are tender. Add mushrooms and cook for about five minutes. Serve cold.

Mushroom Omelet

Sauté the mushrooms in oil and set aside. Beat eggs and cook over a low heat in a skillet with hot oil. When eggs are just set, add most of the mushrooms and parsley. Turn omelet in half and add the remainder of mushrooms on top.

Let Them Eat Flowers

We thoroughly enjoy growing flowers in our indoor hydroponic system. Their fragrance and beauty makes any room a garden.

The flowers we like to grow are ones that are *edible!* I love to use a bunch of pansies in a green salad, nasturtiums in a jello mold or geraniums in a cake. They add delicate flavors and great beauty to a meal and I always feel rather glamorous using them.

There are many outstanding recipes using flowers.

Violets

We have collected volumes on the subject. Here are some of our favorites.

Making Tea

Making flower teas is one delightful use of edible flower petals or leaves. We dry them single-layered, on foil, in a 200° oven. When they are dry, we crumble and store them in airtight jars. Tea is made by steeping one to three teaspoons for each cup of hot water for three to ten minutes according to taste.

Marigolds

One fine flower to grow for the dinner table is the marigold or calendula. It adds color and texture to a dish.

Wash the flowers gently and pull the petals from the flower base.

Prepare marigold petals as a garnish for any meat dish, cream soup, or egg dish by crisping them in ice water.

Marigold

Marigold Cauliflower

> 1 large, whole cauliflower
> ¼ cup butter, melted
> Pinch of salt
> 2 tsp dried marigold petals
> 12 fresh marigold flowers

Cook the whole cauliflower in boiling, salted water, 15-20 minutes until tender but not too soft. Add the dried flower petals during the last seven minutes of cooking, being sure the cauliflower is submerged so it will take on the flower color evenly. Drain and add melted butter. Garnish with fresh flowers.

Marigold Rice

> 3 cups instant rice
> 1 onion, sautéed in butter
> 3 cups bouillon
> ½ tsp parsley
> 3 tsp dried marigold petals

Bring bouillon to a boil. Add rice, onions, parsley and marigolds. Let sit for 15 minutes tightly covered. Stir lightly and serve. (This is even nicer with noninstant brown rice.)

Marigold Scrambled Eggs

> eggs
> cream cheese
> chopped petals

Scramble eggs. Add cream cheese. Just before the eggs are set, add rosemary and marigolds.

Marigold petals may also be used for coloring in mashed potatoes, turnips, dumplings, and salads.

Geraniums

The geranium leaves and flowers are edible. Their taste varies with the variety and color. Experiment to find the flavor that best compliments your food.

Geranium leaves make a pretty garnish for molded salads and hors d'oeuvres.

Geranium Cake

Prepare a white cake batter. Before you pour it into the greased cake pan, arrange the flowers in the bottom, upside down. Then pour in the batter and bake. Cool and serve with powdered sugar.

Crushed geranium leaves make a fragrant flavoring for soups, poultry, fish sauces, custards, and fruit puddings.

Nasturtiums

The nasturtium plant has a subtle, peppery taste. Its young leaves have a mild cress-like flavor which is delicious in salads.

The nasturtium is my favorite cooking flower. The blossoms are delicious in salads and beautiful as garnishes.

Nasturtium seeds appear after the flower has withered and should be picked when green and tender. They make an excellent substitute for capers.

Nasturtium

Nasturtium Salads

Chop flowers and seeds into any raw salad.

Add chopped leaves to a plate of tomatoes, or cucumbers with salt and dill.

Mix chopped leaves with bean salads, cole slaw and tomato, cheese and onion salad.

For a party treat add the flowers to your favorite jello after it has partially set.

Use chopped nasturtium leaves with cold cream soups.

Nasturtium Consommé

Use the blossoms with clear consommé, adding them chopped fine just before serving. Float a blossom and a leaf in each bowl.

Nasturtium Sandwiches

A nasturtium sandwich can be made by sprinkling chopped petals over buttered or cream-cheesed bread. Garnish with a whole blossom.

Nasturtium Appetizers

Fill the flower with cream cheese or a spread for pretty appetizers.

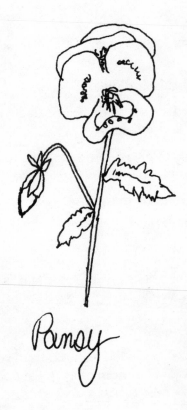

Pansy

Violets and Pansies

The violet and the pansy make delicate and lovely additions to a meal.

Violet leaves are very good added chopped to an omelet garnished with the flower blossoms.

Violet blossoms are also good added to a green salad.

Many more flowers are edible and delicious. However, some are poisonous, so be sure to check a good reference work before cooking with a new flower.

Here is a brief list of some additional flowers that are good to eat:

Carnations
Chrysanthemums
Dandelions
Elder flowers
Fuchsias
Lilies
Primroses
Roses

It's fun to experiment using new flowers in various dishes and inventing your favorite recipes!

Vegetable
Beauty Treatments

One of the most interesting uses for homegrown hydroponic vegetables is in beauty treatments and cosmetics.

Cucumber

Cucumber, which I grow both indoors and out year-round, is excellent as a natural beautifier. It is used as a facial astringent, for blemishes, and for chapped hands. It is also very good for eyes, for oily skin, and for sunburn.

Tightening Cucumber Mask

    1 small peeled cucumber
    ¼ tsp lemon juice or cider vinegar
    1 tsp witch hazel
    1 tsp ethyl alcohol
    1 egg white, beaten

Blend the cucumbers quickly. Add all ingredients. Pat the mixture on your face and allow it to dry for at least 15 minutes.

The cucumber has a hormone which is a good anti-wrinkle aid. You can use a peeled cucumber lathered on the face for a fine skin refresher.

Cucumber Astringent

    1 peeled cucumber, mashed
    1 tsp witch hazel
    1 tsp rose water
    egg white, beaten until frothy
    ¼ tsp honey
    ¼ tsp yogurt

Mix ingredients in a blender or with an electric mixer. Keep the mixture in the refrigerator to apply as desired.

I find that a slice of cucumber on each eyelid will revitalize tired eyes.

Tomatoes

Tomatoes, which I grow in our outdoor hydroponic house, are great for treating oily skin.

Tomato with Lemon Facial

Blend a tomato with lemon juice. Splash it on your face. Sometimes I just rub a half-tomato on my face for a quick skin refresher. Allow it to dry for 15 minutes before you wash it off with tepid water.

Carrots

The best way to use hydroponic carrots as a beauty aid is to eat them! Since you don't need to use pesticides, your carrots will be sweet and delicious. They aid eyesight and are excellent for treating skin problems and allergy attacks.

Carrots make a very good skin care product.

Carrot Juice Facial

To make a carrot juice facial, just mix a carrot in a blender, then add:

whipped egg white, or
honey, or
buttermilk

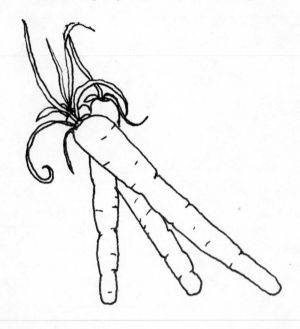

Carrot Eye-Oil For Crow's Feet

Mix a carrot in the blender. Add enough safflower oil to allow the grated carrot to hold to the area around the eyes.

Eating leafy green vegetables provides a natural deodorant. The green leaves are high in chlorophyll. Especially good are:

Parsley
Watercress
Tops of radishes
Tops of beets and turnips
Outside leaves of lettuce

Strawberries also make a fine skin conditioner. Just rub a handful of mashed strawberries on your face, leave on for 10 minutes and wash off.

A cup of milk mixed with the mashed strawberries is an excellent face cleanser. Leave it on at least 10 minutes and wash it off with first warm and then cold water.

Saving a Perfect Flower

Although with our hydroponic system I can grow my favorite flowers all year long, I sometimes enjoy saving a pretty sample of a prize blossom.

Flower preserving is a simple, age-old craft. With a few materials and some favorite flowers you can have a delicate centerpiece for months or years, and a picture that will last indefinitely.

There are four basic methods of flower preserving:

Hanging
Absorption
Drying
Pressing

Hanging

This method is used for fine, thin, small-petaled flowers like baby's breath and bachelor's button.

Pick a bunch of the same kind of flower before fully mature. Strip the stems of all leaves. Tie the ends of the stems lightly and securely with string. Hang them upside down until dry.

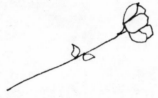

Absorption

Broad leaves and sprays of broad-leaf branches can be preserved in this way:

Fill a tall, thin jar with 1/4 part glycerine, 3/4 part water.

Smash the ends of the stems with a hammer. Leave the smashed ends of the stems in the glycerine solution—in a dark, dry place—for two-three weeks, keeping the water level up.

Drying

Petal flowers like daises, carnations, marigolds, and roses are preserved by this method:

Clean a bucket of sand by sifting it to remove most

of the dirt. Wash it by filling a bucket three-fourths full with sand, and to the top with warm water. Skim off particles, repeat until the water is clean.

Spread the sand out on a sheet to dry. Besides clean, dry sand you will need:

quart size or larger tin can
medium-weight florists wire
green floral tape
tablespoon
small, fine paint brush

Cut the stem three inches from the flower. Put the flower, stem down, in a tin surrounded by sand. Lightly pour sand around the flower and spoon sand over the flower to bury it. In two weeks, or when it feels straw-like, remove it by the stem. Tap it to shed most of the sand, brush off what remains.

Attach to the short stem a length of florists wire, connecting it with green floral tape.

Pressing

Grasses, ferns, and thin flowers may be preserved as a picture by pressing.

Lay a flat sheet of cardboard or corrugated paper on the floor. Spread about five layers of white paper toweling on top. Arrange your flowers and leaves so none touch each other. Spread over them five more layers of paper towels and another layer of cardboard. Place a heavy weight on top. Flowers take about a week to press.

Tarragon

Grow Your Own
Herbs and Spices

One of the greatest hydroponic pleasures is herb growing. Many herbs may be grown successfully indoors, including:

balsam	horse radish	rosemary
borage	lavender	rue
sweet basil	lemon balm	sage
chives	lemon geranium	savory
chervil	lovage	tarragon
dill	marjoram	thyme
fennel	mint	woodruff
garlic	parsley	

Of course, the best way to use these fragrant plants is as spicings for foods. We also use them to make delicious beverage teas. For centuries people have been taking herbal teas (and poultices) for their various medicinal properties as well as their fine flavors.

As with flowers, herb teas are made by drying the herbs in a 200° oven and storing them in airtight jars. Steep one to three teaspoons for each cup for three to ten minutes, according to taste.

We have listed a few of the simple-to-grow, common kitchen herbs and their properties. They can be grown close together in a small indoor hydroponic system.

Herb seeds are available at most nurseries and at all mail-order seed companies.

Several seed companies specialize in the unusual, hard-to-find herb seeds. For their names and addresses see the bibliography.

Herbs and Their Uses

Sweet Basil

Basil

Try finely chopped fresh leaves in scrambled eggs or cheese omelettes. The chopped leaves are also good added to salads. Make a tea for an old herbal remedy to improve the digestion.

Chives

Chopped greens are great added to cream cheese or sour cream for baked potatoes. Try adding fresh leaves to fish, salads, and soups.

Chives

Dill

Most dill plants grown hydroponically do not produce seeds but the greens are very good. By far our favorite use is to add small pieces fresh to tossed salads with an oil and vinegar dressing. The fresh greens are also good in an omelet. Try dill with sautéed mushrooms, stews, new potatoes, fresh peas, and with cucumber slices in yogurt.

Dill

Marjoram

Try chopped leaves on toasted cheese sandwiches. Or add while cooking to fish, veal, and chicken. Made into a tea, marjoram is said to have numerous healthful properties.

Mint

The leafy tops are good in beverages, with fruits, ice cream, jellies, salads and sauces for fish and meats. Mint is said to be good for a stomachache when taken as a tea.

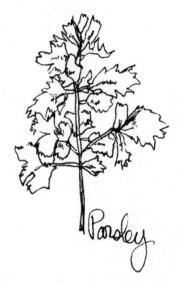

Parsley

This useful herb is very high in iron and potassium and therefore good for anemia and the heart. The leaves are delicious added to white sauce for fish dinners. Make parsley butter by mixing finely chopped greens with soft butter. Grind up the roots and add to salads. We use parsley at almost every meal. They say it is good for the digestion.

Rosemary

Put fresh leaves inside roasting chickens. It is a fine flavoring for apple jelly to be served with roast lamb. Use dried and powdered rosemary as a seasoning for stewed tomatoes. And apply wet leaves to bee stings. The leaves and flowers are also an old fashioned remedy for colds. Rosemary makes a good hair rinse, too.

Rosemary

Sage

This is an excellent seasoning for all poultry dishes and pork. It is also said to impart a quality of "acute mental discernment" when the leaves are taken as a tea.

Summer Savory

Add to stuffing for turkey before roasting. The refreshing tea is good for colds. It is also especially delicious with string beans and fava beans.

Thyme

Use with grilled fish or rub the fresh leaves on meat before roasting. The refreshing tea is good for colds. Try leaves in a cloth bag added to the bath for an especially soothing effect.

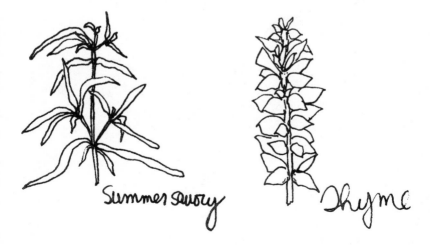

Summer Savory   Thyme

Part V:
Serious Thoughts

Like John, Alexandra, and Lexa Dickerman, your family can do something about its own food needs with easy-to-use hydroponic gardening methods.

John Talks About the
World Food Problem

There has been a lot of talk lately about overpopulation and the possibility of worldwide starvation. Many people have suggested that hydroponics may be a solution to the world's food shortage problem.

There certainly are several advantages of hydroponics over soil gardening. It provides an efficient use of land—hydroponic growing beds produce at least ten times as much food as growing in the same area of soil. Fertilizer and water are used efficiently since they are

An inside peek at a simple home hydroponic greenhouse showing the growing bed (just look at the artichokes, strawberries, and tomatoes!), a fan for cooling and a simple heater for chilly nights.

recycled. And hydroponic gardens are not so vulnerable to changes in the weather.

There are already several thousand commercial hydroponic greenhouses in operation, mostly growing off-season tomatoes, cucumbers, and some lettuce. No doubt there will be increased numbers of commercial hydroponic greenhouses in the future, although for now the main interest is in the off-season and specialty crops.

But at this time the staple of the American diet is not vegetables. We eat mostly grains and meat, both of which require large areas of land to produce. We eat vegetables only as side dishes, which usually take up a small portion of our weekly budget.

It takes about eight to ten pounds of grain to put one pound of meat on a steer of 700 pounds. And it takes 21 pounds of protein in feed to produce one pound of protein in beef cattle. About two-thirds of all the grain we produced in the United States in one recent year went to feed animals.

So, in order to take full advantage of the potential of a hydroponic garden to solve the problem of high food costs and food shortages, our dietary habits would have to change. We would have to eat less beef and more high-protein grains, nuts, seeds, bean sprouts, fish, chicken, and vegetables.

As an additional advantage, this kind of diet, higher in vegetables and lower in beef, could save many American lives. Studies indicate that the high cholesterol menace, high blood pressure, and heart problems would be minimized with a lower consumption of animal fats.

If each family in the United States had a home hydroponic unit in operation we could produce enormous amounts of vegetables—equivalent to about 120,000 acres of choice farm land.

But lifelong habits are hard to break and changing our dietary habits would take time. The home hydroponic system may well be the garden of the future as we gradually become more accustomed to new eating patterns.

Perhaps in the future each family will raise most of its own food. There will be specially bred corn and beans to provide complete proteins and extensive selections of balanced vegetables and fruits for nutrition and variety. Then, for an autonomous food system, a family could have a fish pond and perhaps a chicken coop.

These animal-raising systems, combined with a hydroponic greenhouse, can provide a complete, closed ecological system. The scraps and waste from the greenhouse can feed the fish and chickens. And the animal waste and nonedible parts can be processed to produce fertilizer for the greenhouse.

This complete system could even be solar-powered to provide a family with all its food. We have the technology and the research has already been done to develop autonomous home food supply systems.

Still, the main problem with this plan is a lack of food variety. A family would have to eat beans of some kind daily and perhaps chicken and fish three or four times a week.

So what the future food situation will be probably

depends on all of us. If we experiment with home food producing systems, growing greater portions of our family meals hydroponically, we may find ourselves more secure, economically and nutritionally, in the years to come.

We are sure that your hydroponic garden will be as rewarding and enjoyable for you as ours has been for us. We are all pioneers in this new field and together our efforts and discoveries may provide new resources for our lives and for the generations of the future.

Let us know how your garden is growing. If we may be of help in answering questions, write to John and Alexandra Dickerman in care of the publisher.

baby lexa in her petals

Part VI:
Books and Sources

Other Books
on Hydroponics

Beginner's Guide To Hydroponics by James Douglas; Drake Publishing, 381 Park Ave. S., New York 10016 (1973). An excellent introduction with many good ideas for growing vegetables. Describes manual systems in detail. Nothing on automated systems.

Hydroponic Gardening by Raymond Bridwell, Woodbridge Press, Box 6189, Santa Barbara, Ca., 93111 (1974). Lots of technical information in an easy-to-read style. A must for the home greenhouse owner.

Hydroponics Plus by Maxwell Bentley, P.O. Box 630283, Miami, Florida, 33163. Excellent discussion of hydroponics and semicommercial production.

More Food From Your Garden by Jacob R. Mittleider, Woodbridge Press, Box 6189, Santa Barbara, Ca., 93111. A practical combination of the best aspects of hydroponic and conventional gardening in "grow-box" garden beds. A complete gardening manual.

Soilless Culture by T. Saunby (1953). A classic, available in most libraries. Detailed discussion of growing plants above nutrient solutions in chicken wire beds.

Check your local library under the subjects: "Hydroponics" and "Soilless Culture" for more books.

Gardening Magazines

For new plants to grow and ideas. Probably more about hydroponics in the future.

Plants Alive Magazine, 319 N.E. 45th, Seattle, Wash. 98105. Excellent articles on indoor and greenhouse growing. Good photography.

Horticulture Magazine, 125 Garden St., Marion, Ohio 43302. Lots of information on flowers and vegetables.

Flower & Garden Magazine, 4251 Pennsylvania, Kansas City, Mo. 64111. Good all-around gardening magazine.

Under Glass, Box 114, Irvington, N. Y., 10533. Devoted to greenhouse gardening in general, plus hydroponics.

Avant Gardener, Box 489, New York, N.Y., 10028. Bi-monthly newsletter with latest news on new growing systems and new ideas.

Mail Order
Seed Companies

If your local nursery doesn't have everything you need in the seed and gadget line.

May Seed & Nursery Co., Shenandoah, Iowa.

A good source for seeds, supplies, and gardening equipment.

Mellinger's Inc., 2310 West South Range, North Lima, Ohio 44452.
One thousand assorted pieces of horticultural equipment and seeds, nursery stock and a wonderful catalog. Fast service.

Nichol's Garden Nursery, 1190 N. Pacific Hwy., Albany, Oregon 97321. All kinds of ordinary and strange seeds. Excellent source of herb, spice, wildflower, and vegetable seeds and books on gardening.

Healing Properties of Herbs

The Healing Power Of Herbs by May Bethel, Wilshire Book Co., Los Angeles, Ca. (1974).

A Modern Herbal by M. Grieve, Dover Press, New York, N.Y. (1967).

Book Of Herb Lore by Lady Rosaland Worthcote, Dover Press, New York, N.Y. (1971).

Herbal Remedies by Simmonite and Culpepper, Foulsham & Co. Ltd., London (1957).

Back To Eden by Jethro Kloss, Lifeline Books, Box 6189, Santa Barbara, Ca. (1939, 1975).

Growing Mushrooms

Mushroom Growing For Everyone by Roy Genders, Faber & Faber, London (1969).

A Little More Light

The Complete Book Of Gardening Under Lights by E. McDonald, Popular Library, New York, N.Y. (1965).

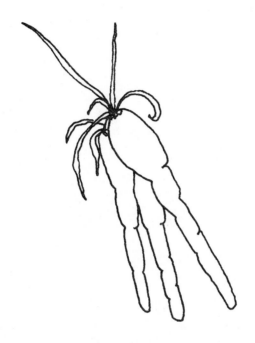

More for Your Face

Here's Egg On Your Face Or How To Make Your Own Cosmetics by Beatrice Traven, Pocket Books, New York, N.Y.

Mother Nature's Beauty Cupboard by Donna Lawson, Bantam Books, New York, N.Y. (1973).

The Complete Herbal Guide to Natural Health And Beauty by D. D. Buchman, Doubleday, New York, N.Y. (1973).

Cooking With Flowers

Cooking With Flowers by Zack Hanle, Price/Stern/Sloan, Los Angeles, Ca. (1971).

The Art Of Cooking With Herbs And Spices by Milorodovich, Doubleday, NewYork, N.Y. (1952).

Gardening And Cooking On Terrace And Patio by D. Hogner, Doubleday, New York, N.Y. (1964).

Hydroponic Supplies
and Equipment

The best information we have at this time. Will be happy to include other established sources in future printings if you will tell us about them. Remember, too, that you can get much of what you need for hydroponics at well-stocked farm, garden, and nursery shops everywhere. Also check your local yellow pages under: hydroponics, greenhouses, gardening, pumps, timers, seeds, plastics and plastic trays, etc.

Acorn Horticultural Equipment, 1812 Laguna St., Santa Barbara, California 93101.

Aqua-Gro, Inc., Box 827, Powell, Wyoming 82435.

Aero Hydroponics, 5366 Jackson Drive, La Mesa, California 92041.

Aquaponics, 22135 Ventura Blvd., Woodland Hills, California 91364.

Aquaponics, 1020 E. Vermont, Anaheim, California 92805.

The Biosphere, 2821 N.E. 55th St., Seattle, Washington 98105.

Burwell Geoponics Corp., Box 125, Rancho Santa Fe, Calif. 92067.

Casey Hydroponics, Box 1121, Wilkes-Barre, Pennsylvania 18701.

Dr. Chatalier's Plant Food Co., Box 20375, St. Petersburg, Florida 33742.

Bridwell Hydroponic Mix, Box 192, Perris, California 92370.

Bel-Mor Distributing Co., 3600 Pama Lane, Las Vegas, Nevada 89120.

Continental Nutriculture, Box 6751, Lubbock, Texas 79413.

Environmental Dynamics, Box 996, Sunnymead, California 92388.

Evergreen Hydroponics, 637 West Holt Ave., Pomona, California 91768.

Ferro Greenhouse Systems, 2 Binnacle, Mount Harmony, Maryland 20836.

Gro-Master Hydroponics, McKee Road, Box E, Collegedale, Tennessee 37315.

Home-Grow, Inc., Box 2002, Akron, Ohio 44309.

HHH Horticultural, 68 Brooktree Road, Hightstown, N.J. 08520.

Hudson's Garden Center, 12031 Beach Blvd., Stanton, California 90680.

Hydro House, 425 Garden St., Santa Barbara, California 93101.

Hydro House of the Bay, 808 San Antonio Rd., Palo Alto, California 94303.

Hydro-Gardens, Inc., Box 9707, Colorado Springs, Colorado 80932.

Hydro-Magic Gardens, 1349 Regent St., Alameda, California 94501.

Hydrome Industries, 19634 Ventura Blvd., Tarzana, California 91356.

Hydroponic Chemical Company, Copley, Ohio 44321.

Hydroponic and Greenhouse Supplies, Division of E.R.I., Inc., 6433 Sepulveda Blvd., Van Nuys, California 91401.

Hydroponics Corp. of America, 745 Fifth Ave., New York City, New York 10022.

The Hydroponics Company, Box 191, Little Rock, Arkansas 72203.

Hydroponics Hobbies, 105 N. Edison Way #2, Reno, Nevada 89502.

Hydroponic Industries, Inc. 5650 S. Syracuse Circle, Englewood, Colorado 80110.

McLean Associates, 10885-G Kalawa River Ave., Fountain Valley, California 92708.

Mellinger's, Inc., 2310 West South Range, North Lima, Ohio 44452.

Modular Hydroponic Gardens, Box 812, Fountain Valley, California 92708.

Nichol's Garden Nursery, 1190 North Pacific Highway, Albany, Oregon 97321.

Nutri-Gardens Greenhouse, 2000 Portola Rd., Woodside, California 94062.

Pacific Coast Greenhouse Co., 430 Burlingame Ave., Redwood City, California 94063.

Redwood Domes, Box 666, Aptos, California 95003.

Southern Greenhouse Builders, 2935 Powell Ave., Nashville, Tennessee 37204.

Texas Greenhouse Co., 2717 St. Louis Ave., Fort Worth, Texas 76110.

Wondergrow Farms, 2953 Deerfield St., Lakewood, California 90712.

Fleetwood Nursery, 7422 Garden Grove Blvd., Westminster, California 92683.

Typography: Friedrich Typography
Santa Barbara, California

Printing and Binding:
Griffin Printing and Lithograph
Glendale, California